Deliver Me From Evil

A collection of poetry

James M. Mckay

The poetry contained in this book is a collection of poems I have written over the course of fourteen years.

You will notice how a lot of it is dark and depressing. The newer poetry takes on a more positive role.

I lived most of my life battling the man in the mirror at my own cost. It wasn't until October of 2009 that the battle finally ended. In the end, Jesus saved me.

I chose to go ahead and put it all in, the good and the bad... and some a bit ugly too. It was all part of the battle between the man I was and the man I have become.

It has always been one of my dreams to publish my poetry... the very thing that has helped me cope with life... so here goes.

God bless.

-M

Life

1998

- I once was a child with a care free mind
- I thought nothing of my friends leaving me behind
- As I grew older, things began to change
- When my friends left me, I suddenly felt strange
- It was then I realized I was no longer a boy
- I must pursue a goal to bring myself joy
- As I settled down I thought of taking a wife
- This is were commitment came into my life
- When I became a father I was the proudest man on earth

- To a beautiful little child, my wife had given birth
- Now all is said and done, and I am glad
- What a wonderful life that I have had

Silver moons

1997

- Slipping away into a land unknown
- Giving the love , which forever, you own
- Holding onto silver moons of love
- Floating away to the heavens above
- Smiles of sadness on my heart strung face
- As you glitter my soul with passion and grace
- The reflection of my love lives without end
- Silver moons show the roads on which I begin
- A long journey for a love desired
- Great passions, silver moons have inspired

- To have the love I see in your eyes
- Rejecting deception of lustful lies
- Silver moons hold hearts made of gold
- And in the silver moons are my confessions untold

Moon of hope

1997

- The sun is fading the moon away
- It disappears for yet another day
- The brightness of its light driving away the night
- Pink and orange colors fill my eyes sight
- Touching your lips so softly, but not waking you
- Getting lost in the worlds sky, so blue
- Wishing for the love you so strongly desire
- But a cold shall fall over my burning fire
- Shadows cast by the moon; its own master
- As falling stars become a disaster

- The sun must fall for the moon to rise
- As my heart hangs in the glittered skies
- Sold away by the lies that kill
- Holding back tears, not knowing what to feel
- The moon is not alone, for it has many peers
- The stars, in which I wish away my fears
- So lost, I think that I know the way
- And losing the thoughts that I fear to say
- Let's see what awaits in my moon of hope today.

I am Rage
1997

- My rage is calmed in a sea of tranquility
- And to what do I owe for this seemingly gentle breeze
- Stopping the storm before its hate begins to pour down
- As it always has, like the piercing evidence of our sins
- But not all is as it appears to be on the surface
- For our gentle breeze shall quickly grow untamed
- To control my rage I must live silent with my love
- Love is only above hate, love that repairs any heart

- But hate... hate can destroy anyone
- Assuring myself that all the beauty I seek
- All the beauty, choked in black, with tempting eyes and a silver neck
- That this beauty is worth it
- Worth the suffering of my trapped rage
- Waiting for its chance to escape the mind I've imprisoned it in
- But to see this desire and let it go without word would be as foolish as battling the rage without faith
- But what is faith? Faith is just some hope, and it can't help

me to defeat what I fear to believe

- As my sins sting my skin with the punishment that I have always deserved
- The calmness shall depart, and rage shall take over
- That is when I will no longer be myself
- Now I must face emptiness with tranquility behind
- To reach for the beauty wrapped in a strain of leather
- Symbolic silver symbolizing the love
- The only thing to calm the rage
- If the love is forever lost
- My name will forever be rage

Together
1997

- Dark embers fading in lovely starlit smiles
- Beautiful dreams in many heart felt styles
- Making love in the rain
- Forever dreaming and forgetting the pain
- Forgotten speeches of promises made
- In my heart is where your love stayed
- Togetherness is blessed, and together we are one
- Loving together beneath the moon and sun
- Sleeping still and stealing kisses
- Not being held back by forever misses

- Slipping away into your land of dreams
- Slowly watching the world as your heart sings
- And always knowing where your love lies
- Enchanted in the realm of my eyes

Letting out the rain

1997

- All my anger, all my fears, I have kept in me all these years

- Living in a world of sadness, drowning in all my tears

- Moonlight shinning through the cracks of my prayers

- Not wanting to follow where my lonely heart dares

- Sending a message that everything is fine

- My broken heart may heal in time

- The stars in my skies are the stars in your eyes

- Embracing every bit of love and not rejecting it with lies

- Spilled over emotions dripping from my cup

- But sadness fails as your wings of love lift me up

- Recovering softly spoken words, unknown how to say
- Following my love struck heart, unaware, day by day
- Slipping through the holes in my net of thoughts are my dreams
- I find myself falling in love, or so it seems
- And all I ever wanted was to feel the way I do
- My mind is a lot of nonsense and my heart belongs to you
- Swimming in your ocean of beauty, your soft lips I caress
- Glittered by the thought of it, as I give my heart for you to bless
- I know I cannot make it rain, not even a little bit
- But I still feel that sinking feeling, and I'm in love with it
- It's the feeling of my heart sinking into your hands

- Giving all the love that this love demands
- Following the moon and stars, they will lead me to my place
- And know what it means to never lose love, and never fall from grace

The draining syndrome
2000

- The draining syndrome
- Forgetting not what you said
- Blame it all on what I lose
- Repetition of failure
- When I succeed you take away
- Drawn in by my love for you
- Sketched   upon   me   is inconsistency
- You are everything I last for
- So   beautiful;   you   don't understand
- I am living in your heart
- Who am I to love you?
- In my heart you are forever mine
- Am I the one you love?
- Meaning to be meant to be
- To die for you

- Inspiring to me
- For the last time I last for
- The draining syndrome of life
- Of love.

Departure of thy Start light Love
1997

- Sweet memories of things in the past
- Even in our dreams, our love can never last
- 'parting is such sweet sorrow', a poet once said
- Your image forever drifting in my lonely head
- A love that can take us to higher ground
- Was our star light love, never to be found
- What could have been may never be
- For star light love has abandoned me
- The things you say, so sweet to my ears

- Your beautiful smile chases away my fears
- Lost in your eyes, wondering where it would end
- Not knowing you would depart just as a friend
- You meant more than you will ever know
- And my star light love, forever, continues to grow

Return of thy Star Light Love

1997

- To be graced with the love I thought I'd never have; as if in a dream
- My heart overjoyed by the presence of your beauty; floating in loves stream
- I hold you close and it feels so right
- As we carry our love into the light
- You have come back and we have found true love
- For you I give thanks to the Lord above
- forever under the stars we shall dance
- I pray for no end to our romance
- I will give you all my love and whatever you desire

- Our hearts fueling our passions fire
- Star light love, forever, we shall share
- As we tend our love with star light care
- Even in my arms, we are still too far apart
- Let us hold tight to star light love, and we shall never part

Don't Let Go
1998

- With one touch; with one kiss
- Your love shall never deceive my wish
- To finally find true love is grand
- It is the feeling I get when I touch your hand
- I will love you forever, and even longer
- Day by day, our love grows stronger
- I am forever faithful, for you give me reason to live
- The velvet skies are the limit on the love I give
- Do not ever let go, and we will hold on for good
- I am loving you like I never knew I could

- You found a lost soul and gave me love
- I have been lifted higher than the heavens above
- I love you more with every breath I take
- So forever love me, for my hearts sake
- Your sweet face and beautiful eyes
- Have imprisoned my love in your lavender skies
- But I do not struggle; or try to break free
- For I love you more than any eye can see
- And will always love you
- So don't let go.

Tales of a Homeless Soul

1997

- Walking past the frozen pond on a chilly winter night
- Everything in from the cold; not a soul in sight
- The cold night wind is blue as it blows through the lands
- In need of a warm fire to thaw my frozen hands
- Pushing forward through the snow
- All alone, with no place to go
- Blue are my lips, as blue as the ice
- Dirty gloves and a coatless back will have to suffice
- I have been on my own for much too long
- And running out of lyrics for my sad song

- Place to place, I travel alone
- Sleeping on the ground with a chill in my bone
- Wondering what day will be my last
- Wishing I could change what's in the past
- Going unnoticed, but receiving an often glance
- As starvation takes over, my thoughts begin to dance
- No one to love, and no one to be loved by
- And no one can hear my lonesome cry.

What She Fears To Hear
1997

- The flattery which once charmed her soul now grates harshly upon her ear
- And all the truths that are told are the fears she fears to hear
- Raining silently on her mind
- And she is unaware that she is running out of time.

The Other Side of the Silver Moon
1997

- What would your heart say if silver were its only color
- We lost it here today, because grey is much duller
- Do not lie to thy silver moon
- Do not serve it grey on a silver spoon
- For grey cannot withstand the fame
- The fame that gave silver its name
- One half is dark; one half is light
- But it is always silver as it moves through the night
- Never changing or loosing its shine
- Sending cold shivers down your spine

- Always hanging on to this silver moon of love
- Never loosing the shine it was given from above
- Bright silver will forever shine
- Laying grey flowers on this silver heart of mine

Hold on to thy Love so True
1998

- For the lost thoughts your soul cannot find

- To every whisper that enters your mind

- Your heart may feel that kind of touch

- There is no turning back when you love so much

- For that ordinary heart that feels your pain

- To every lover who has tasted silver rain

- Keep faith and your heart shall stay strong

- With a faith so loving you can't go wrong

- And every murmur, so hard to understand

- Will not love you and leave you; heart in hand

- For one day love shall find you; no longer shall you be lost

- And you shall hold onto that love, forever, at any cost
- For your sweetheart, so deeply desired
- Giving you wings of love and setting your heart afire
- With a burning love no one can deny
- And with a tempting grace no one can defy
- Once forever lost; but shall be no more
- True love hath cometh to knock on your door
- Answer it gracefully, with star light in your eyes
- Your love shall grow strong under our sorrow skies
- Rescue your love from the demons at hand
- For your true love, take the final stand
- The hellish hardships will be worth the prize
- For you have fought for a love of great size

- I will be here with you, until we fall from grace
- And only then, shall heaven be our place
- For heaven on earth is what we have now
- Letting love love me, as only love knows how
- In my mind I see your face
- Our hearts are in the same place
- So keep thy love true
- And remember... I love you.

Starlight Love

1996

- In the satin sheets we roll, Under our blanket skies

- In the heat of passion we whisper love filled lies

- And forever under the stars we shall dance

- And pray for no end to our romance

- For if love is happiness

- Then we have it all

- Up in our star filled skies

- From grace we shall never fall

- My love for you will forever remain

- And your love in return I hope to gain

- The rain comes down, The steam comes up

- Our passion overflowing like wine from a cup

- My heart throbs deep for you to be near

- I will love you always and forever my dear.

Falling from grace
1998

- Many dark nights ago
- Beyond the shadows and past my fears
- The cold wind began to blow
- Rustling leaves, whistling in my ears
- I felt my blood begin to warm, despite the ice in the air
- I knew I could not run from harm, or escape the looks of evils cold stare
- So with nothing else to do, I began to cry
- All the sadness was just too much
- In my heart I only wanted to die
- But my love would never allow me such

- And the darkness circles around my mind
- And all my failures are driving me blind
- So I stay awake until I die
- Just to leave the world wondering why.

The Rose

2000

- The rose did not arrive in time
- In time to save love
- As it was gracefully given to me
- It is brutally taken from above
- My tears and sorrow cannot hide
- I fade from her life now
- The rose was late- but was it the reason?
- I merely use it as a symbol, the only way I know how
- To represent my mistakes, my loss and pain
- I have lost her... and with this I cry
- Hurt again...it is always me
- I love her... without her I die
- Surely, slowly, I will recover
- With yet another hole in my heart
- In love with her always- saddened that were apart

- Distant sadness follows my present grief
- I try so hard but still I fail
- I feel like I cannot breathe
- Drowning in the love that I fell
- I look at her and see perfection
- To me, she is as perfect as can be
- I hate that I love her, for what she's doing to me
- I look into my future and deception is all I see
- She does not love me anymore
- Perhaps she has found another soul
- But I will always send her my love
- From my dark and lonely hole
- My mind and heart are broken
- I cry inside and out
- I cannot take the truth, so I tell myself lies
- I love her I know, without a doubt
- But she fell out of love with me
- I was not what she wanted after all
- I strangle my words with pain

- From nothing I will always fall
- All I had to offer was my love
- And this single rose
- But the rose was late and my love was not enough
- She loves me not, so off she goes
- Maybe I ruined the best thing in my life
- Maybe it was not meant to be
- But I still love her
- And wish she still loved me

- Worthless rose.

- It died.

Spoil

2001

- Cold night rushes through skin
- Descending rain makes me cold within
- Dying light- dimming in your eyes
- At the end of our road we see the reflection of our lies
- Sanity is a virtue now missed
- I couldn't see this far when we first kissed
- Our lips met- we became one
- Outstanding expiration- when will this be done?
- Peering behind closed doors you'll see
- No forced tears- no fake smiles on me
- Depending on the swing of my mood
- Being polite, so not to be rude
- Hate of myself now grows within
- When do we get to be ourselves again?

- Shed some light on this helpless fight
- Help me see what's wrong and right
- Make me feel like I belong
- I haven't felt that in so long
- Those misspent days I miss so much
- Endless nights I dream to touch
- Something bright- designed for me
- I feel as though I've ceased to be
- All my hate I love to boast
- Of all I know, I hate me the most.

Passionate Friendship

2000

- I wrote it in the dirt, I wrote it in the sand

- I felt her through my finger tips, and into my hand

- Throughout my body, especially in my heart

- Not wanting it to stop from the start

- Her beauty in and out amazes me to say the least

- And if they can't be again, these experiences I gained at least

- A true friend I have found and will forever hold dear

- Close to my heart, I hold her so near

- Unlike that night, things cant be the way they were

- I still feel so lucky to have a friend like her

Untitled

2001

- Dark and black on a starry night
- I wish I may, I wish I might
- Escape the nightmare that tortures me tonight
- As I cry my tears and battle my demons
- On a night that I deal with these melodramatic feelings
- A sense of calm rushes over my body as cold sets in
- Lost between somewhere and nowhere
- In that grey area... where I still don't fit in.

Sorrow Pusher

2000

- A foul hatred I boil for you, wretched sorrow pusher of tomorrows

- Your empty minds stuck in a useless insecurity mode

- Your conformed eyes only see the lies you tell yourself

- To make yourself forget the emptiness you trap inside

- Belittle others for the sake of your own pitiful insecurities

- Your blaspheming mouth spews vile, disgusting tones

- You smile, both in vain and stupidity

- You laugh so that you may ignore your own cries

- You are no better than the sorrows you push on others

- You...the sorrow pusher.

Unborn

2001

- The loss of a life that I loved before it lived has struck me with a pain in my heart and confusion in my head

- Ready, yet unprepared, I stood with the angel I hold dear, contemplating choices- not knowing that a choice would be made for me

- Maybe it is easier this way- now we'll never know

- As I hold tightly to the feelings I cannot show

- What do I say to the child I never knew?

- To the baby we never had?

- Did that child know the plans that had been laid before the choice was made for us?

- That child will never know how badly I wanted to its father.

- The child I never knew

- The parents it never knew

- The love we were never able to give... unborn

Beginning of the End of the Last Voice
2001

- Rolling off my tongue are my words
- In my head is your voice
- This is the whisper in your ear
- I see your eyes in mine
- My disposition puts me down
- Under the surface of your thoughts
- I have your taste in my mouth
- I tend to spit out the lies
- Desperate for changing- you live
- Deep in my head, I swim
- Tasting your own tears, you change
- I have the hate in me
- Twisted illusions- driving me
- As I touch the hand of bliss
- You cannot stop the feelings
- You cannot change the anger inside me
- My frustration breaks me
- And I hide it well
- Left with nothing- forced to remember

- Tortured by nightmares when I sleep

- Mind twisting creations- do I make

- I tightly grip the spoon of words and chew them up

- I spit them out- there you stand

- Sadistic in my head- I see pain

- Silver necked nooses suffocate words

- Words in voices- haunting me

- Kill the members of your mind

- Create your own scapegoat of me

- Out of the corner of my eye

- I see a blurry vision coming clear

- Rain washes my face

- Cleansed of over dosed conversations

- I still awake to new days.

Hurt

2002

- In the center of my world lies my hurt, hidden amongst the grey clouds, which hang like aged curtains...

- If you can see past the heavy rain that never ceases, maybe you can peer into the face of hurt

- Holding hands with hate...

- In the center, in control... side by side with my insecurity

- Not a place I am able to live at peace in... down rough roads, I try to lose it... leave it all behind, with no success

- It is a world I am all alone in... around every corner I study, searching for a deeper place to push into...

- Yet I cannot even seem to find my way... allowing hurt to tug my leash and drag me forward.

Pushing Buttons
2002

- When caught... regrets that you met me will overcome you

- This hate boils... and you are sentenced to boil in it

- Out of the darkness I climb... lighting my way will be this fire inside

- Unexpectedly, you lose- from my hand I blow your ashes

- I will give you peace... no longer will you worry... thoughts of me can disappear

- All this fueled by my insecurity, which in turns triggers hate... causing a violent reaction

- A fire that no rain can put out

- But yours can be easily extinguished

- Watch over yourself... do not cross the line that I draw... for the floor will open its jaws and devour you, and there you will stay

- Tormented in the stomach of my sorrow

The Battle Within

2002

- At times I feel totally abstract

- As if my soul were showing

- From what I accumulate, the world isn't really against me

- The acrimonious what I go about certain things sends my mind into a frenzy- trying to separate my thoughts in an attempt to figure myself out

- I gaze into a mirror- starring down my adversary, trying to make him blink first

- Never receiving any affable looks- only the cold gaze- the same as the one he receives

- It leaves me totally aghast to realize that I can't beat him

- The amalgamation of anger and insecurity I hold within fuels a hatred for the reflection

- And the altercation continues

- The intense suffering I seem to love to put myself through is just another sting- driving my animosity- therefore I continue to hold grudges against myself

- My mind seems impervious at any attempt to reconcile my own differences

- And my own iniquities bring shame upon me

- Still I wander forward- trying to pick through the debris of thought

- Now here in these words I exploit myself and in turn, I recant my hatred for me

- But only sometimes

- At times I indulge in who I am and rejoice inside

- Merely looking down on sophomoric test dummies.

DreamKillThought
2003

- Here in my head is where the film plays
- Deep within, it withers away
- I am with nothing and left in dismay
- So I decided to kill one of my thoughts today
- In the midst of this battle within
- I forgot to remind myself to breath again
- As I began to choke, I hear your voice
- Insisting that I have no choice
- Then I wake and I'm covered in sweat
- And all I feel inside is regret
- So I lay awake, hour after hour
- I tell myself to take a shower
- Try to wash away the residue of such a dream
- In the dark a thousand eyes gleam
- Now I know I'm still asleep
- Pushing my way through thoughts so deep
-

In That Moment

2002

- In that moment, the world surrounding me disappears
- In that moment, fairytales were reality
- In that moment, new hope actually felt hopeful
- In that moment we existed alone on earth
- In that moment I couldn't remember my name
- In that moment I had no worries
- In that moment, I was lost and found-all at once
- In that moment, white walls changed to blue and I was full of emotion
- It is in that moment, I would like to remember life.

Abstract Mind

2002

- Wake up to a glare- thoughts, here today, gone tomorrow
- Nothing is routine unless it's taken for granted
- Dull pennies hold my eyes- bright colors distract my vision
- Can I read the words etched upon your heart?
- Backwards blue, faded through paper
- Liquid surface- like revolving disc or tops that don't spin
- Bright white are the empty eyes that cover our truths
- Hold onto your true friends- they will be the only family you believe in
- Inspire yourself for the sake of inspiring others- and in turn, gaining inspiration from them
- Ignore broken voices in your head and wake up
- This is no dream. This is my voice. My only voice. And it says to you... believe.

The Lonely Dragon
2003

- Here in a lonely moment, the dragon is surrounded by shadows
- Time ticks away as the thought flow steady
- Smoke billows from his chimney, filling the air with a familiar scent
- He faintly remembers falling asleep- starring into the sun
- Yet he awakes alone- another day, another year
- Nothing but numbers in his journey; a journey with an unknown destination
- The tears in the dragons eyes will never fall
- Even though each step is as painful as the one before

- Surrounded by adversity, he carries on

- Broken hearted and alone- but with the virtue of patience

- The dragon awaits the nights of falling asleep- starring at the sun

- Branded with his own little number he waits

- He awaits the day when he will be seen and heard... and loved.

Out of Reach

2003

- I can't trust in my own fate
- I live with all the things I hate
- It's bottled up so deep inside
- I feel the pain but cannot cry
- All my tears are dried and gone
- As I am forced to live alone
- All my thoughts burn in my head
- As I access the things you've said
- Cannot put feelings aside
- A part of me has already died
- And now the truth will unfurl
- I am in love with this girl
- And there is nothing I can do
- Still I must see feelings through
- I feel so helpless and so weak
-]in this secret that I keep
- I force myself to go on like everything's ok
- I await the days I see you

- Yet I'm scared to speak the truth
- And you always make me smile
- And I haven't kissed you in awhile
- And I live without my beating heart
- You've held that from the start
- Now I hang myself again
- Like the war on me will never end
- The things I cant have cut me deep
- So I hold you tight in dreams as I sleep

The Moon has me

2003

- Pages with smeared ink
- Wrinkled little words faded by fallen tears
- Tortured little voices- from a distance- screaming into the void of midnight
- Gliding in on wings of despair
- Ride feelings of immense stature
- Stacked emotions shackling the voice of reason
- The hands of God tied around my tongue
- Willingly, I lay still
- The moon hangs untouchable- a mirror too far away to see my reflection in… and I am thankful.

Untitled2
2002

- Exiled in my room
- Back again- alone and faced with only me
- I recognize the lonely feeling that I seem to wrap myself in
- I try to overturn
- Turning myself into stone with every breath I take
- And deeper I sink- falling downward
- Into an instant aggression
- And there- in that instant- I lose the world I'm in
- In that instant I hide myself
- So that you think I'm gone.

No Matter

2004

- The grin inside my head- gritting his teeth at me- watching me with haunting eyes

- Anticipating my failure

- Trapped behind glass- like a fish in a bowl

- Waiting for the chance to shatter the glass and spill its own blood

- A desperate act of one who's run out of options- nothing left

- Yet... no matter how far over the edge I dangle- I never beg

- No matter how hard I'm pushed- I never break

- Sometimes I need clarity on why I resist.

As I Break Away

2003

- As I break away from all this distraction
- Pushing buttons just to get a reaction
- Testing the patience of a mind so torn
- Holding back- till my child is born
- So many problems you have with expressing yourself
- I wish that you could just sit next to yourself
- Through the eyes of the viewer
- As the people around you become fewer and fewer
- All the distance you put between myself and you
- I can't change it
- You act like you don't want me to.

Disconnected

2003

- Out of flesh- I stand unnoticed
- The screams echo from wall to wall
- Tear drops fall and crash like shattering glass
- Broken pieces cut my skin
- Open wounds- my life fades so quietly away
- With nothing left to feel, I abandon myself
- I stand, holding my own hand
- Living with the fact that I'm falling again
- The numbness inside begins to feel so comforting
- There I drag myself under, losing breath- I withdraw from the fight, accept sorrow and let it wash over me
- And pray for a chance to start over.

Tearing into me

2002

- With a hatred so omnivorous, I brutally lunge myself forward
- My fists clenched- shattering my glass of thought
- I awake myself from dreams to wish I were still sleeping
- Like greedy profiteers, my thoughts consume me- leaving me with nothing but tangled confusion
- Remonstrating my own remorse, even while it swallows me whole
- I live in this shell, surrendering to every day life- without choice
- I feel as though I am both against myself and my biggest supporter
- Feeling swoon, I calm my nerves
- My nerves seem to fail me
- Growing weaker by the day, falling target to anger

- I transcend my own mind, venturing into a realm of endless possibilities and mishaps
- Thoughts get so twisted I have to temporarily suspend the hostility towards myself to catch my breath
- Yet I cannot seem to make the suspension last
- The uncouth way I fight my feelings drives me insane
- Therefore I bury my feelings deep and hold onto sorrow- caged in anger
- And I still have the nerve to ponder the question...
- Why can I not find happiness?

I feel exactly like I do inside
2002

- I hear the voices, so many voices
- Out of the darkness calls my own
- Where in spiraling sorrow lies my soul
- Building up to the flame- to the release
- To the recollection of a memory I thought I'd lost
- I lose sight of a vision that I can't remember if I ever had
- He hole I hide in is so obvious
- Inside of you/ inside of me
- Delusions/ illusions/ dreams/ reality
- Nothing makes sense- isn't someone listening?
- Words can't be clear- silence is so loud
- So loud
- Default my tears- they never happened

- The words still won't come out right
- Can't find a language for the speechless
- Please again for the last time- until the next
- How pathetic
- The drowning effect begins to take place
- Breath in the sadness
- My own is all I have, if I truly have that
- I continue to break/ I continue to bleed
- Remember life the way it was in the moment you wish you wouldn't have lost.

Fall away

2002

- There was a time you knew me
- But that time passed and you forgot your past
- Like a phase or trendy fad- I fell away
- Home is a fairy tale and the make believe dragon stands alone
- Dragon wings carry me to a story book where you believe in me
- One with happy endings- where I didn't fall away
- Reality is where the tears in my eyes blind me
- Like an aged rose- I crumbled, now I don't exist... and no one remembers the fragile pedals
- The dragon bows his head and forces each step towards smiling faces
- Only to fall away
- Just want someone to believe in me
- Falling rain- a reminder of all those times I drown

- Slipping of the edge are the thoughts the weight me down

- Alone inside my circle of fire

- Looking for a higher place, only from which, to fall away again

- All I can picture are empty smiles

- Only wanting someone to remember the dragon.

Initials

2002

- Years ago the knife was set in place
- Things change, you faded away
- The knife continues to turn
- I begin to understand the pain
- I begin to be my pain
- I begin to enjoy the muffled screams in my head
- I begin to hate things I once loved
- I begin to come to terms with the monster you turned me into
- I feel the pain again and again- like crashing waves
- I begin to picture your face
- I begin to see your breath running short
- I begin to realize that I am still in love with you
- I begin to get a grip on the fact that I hate you
- I begin to see that I needed you

- Now I understand what's happened-
how I let you break my heart

- How you saved me and destroyed me
all at once

- You've made me doubt myself

- Your ghost will haunt me until mine
haunts you

- I will never be ok. I hate you for that

- I myself- am not even worthy of hate.

I feel so alone

2002

- This is desolation- this is the way I feel
- This is what happens when you find out nothings real
- Everyone is fake and my anger begins to grow
- Slowly, happiness fades, and sorrows all I know
- I hate this feeling of being alone- I don't know why it haunts me so much
- I would prefer a frown over fake smiles- in my mind I can't deal with such
- Mixed colors and spiraling thoughts all intertwine in my head
- Unable to shake this feeling of dread
- Fading or falling or just being pushed- either way I'll still be gone
- So you can avoid seeing me and I can be alone.

This is mine

2002

- The past is the past and I can't change what is done

- I'm so weary and tired, and have such a distance left to go

- I deal with now- and try to hold no grudges

- And only my scars remind me of the suffering I have endured and the pain that awaits me ahead.

Starring into a cracked mirror

2002

- To make this go away I push it all inside
- I hate knowing me so well- and everything so well
- And would it be easier not knowing?
- I wouldn't have to care
- I stand alone so strong- yet it tears me apart inside
- And all my guilt is too much
- I always smile at myself, but in that smile I say so much
- I despise so many things in me
- How do I manage to unravel things wrapped up so tight?
- I just want things to go away
- I miss so many things that are already gone
- It's useless to try to be happy- I always make sure I'm not

- Inside I have so many things I don't need
- I lack the ones I do
- And they suffocate me every night
- I just need something or someone- I've never been able to figure out who or what that is
- I'm no help- I only add to my scars
- And I help you add to them as well
- Then I disappear, and you move on.

No Entry

2002

- each day passes like the calm before the storm

- the cold sets in- strange enough- I'm content

- see- through, dirty white, with tiny cracks on the surface

- grey peering through- becoming a world in its own

- my throne grows weary on unsturdy legs

- I peer out a door- left open by accident

- I peer into a gloomy world where no one exists

- Feelings float like a breeze swallowed in emptiness

- The tears are unstoppable- I feel like this

- The distant whisper teasing that it knows things I don't

- Sees things I can't see, hears all that I miss, is where I'll never be

- But above all else- feels the things I only dream about

I hold myself back
2002/2003

- Desperately wandering from place to place
- Sometimes I feel like a man with no face
- I feel as though I'm gifted- yet I don't know how
- I feel the eyes upon me- they're watching me right now
- And every time I raise my arm they're there to pull it down
- All the while I'm screaming out loud
- Without making a sound
- All the while I struggle- with all this pain inside
- I carry your memory with me
- Locked within my mind

Funeral for my thought

2003

- Foul mouths and fortunes played
- One of my thoughts died today
- Deep in my head
- It rotted away
- One of my thoughts died today
- Fair well thought

The end
2003

- Lay down my fears; lay down my pains
- Search through my ashes to find what remains
- I won't be happy with what I find
- There is very little asides that in my mind
- I have the repetitive dream that I'm going to be alone
- This decision that plagues me is the worst I've ever known
- And how it came to this, I still don't have a clue
- At one time, it was the greatest love I ever knew
- I know now that its gone and we'll never get it back
- I'm unsure of what happened to the feelings I lack
- I've never been afraid of lonliness- it's a feeling new to me

- Seems nothing I ever want is ever meant to be
- I wish I could change the way I feel and relight the flame
- Unfortunately I can't- so I will take the blame
- My tears fall as I realize I can't win
- But you'll be better off in the end
- I'll only hold you back, I'll only hold you down
- And in the end... I'll be alone when I drown.

The smell of December

2003

- Sliding down the back of aggression
- Presenting to myself a simple suggestion
- To be myself and shake the fake
- Try to believe in the choices I make
- Try to hold on to a bit of pride
- Stay close to those in whom I confide
- All at once I pray I've forgotten
- All the hardships my life has begotten
- But all those things I only remember
- Unforgettable- like the smell of December
- I see a chance in your eyes- I should force myself to take it
- My intention are real- there's no way to fake it
- These mystic spiraling thoughts tend to make me sway
- I would have it no other way

- Feeling swoon... I stare into the mirror again
- Against me- myself I defend
- Sometimes things can't change when past pains bring sorrow
- And days from now I'll be unable to forget tomorrow
- Just like I remember the smell of December

The separating door and hearts vacant
2003

- You feel so powerless... and you look so weak to me
- Close the blinds on the sun... and shutter at the thought of things to be
- Trapped within such a confined space
- Unable to find the beginning of the steps you retrace
- On the other side of the door, I lock myself within
- My heart caged in armor- so no one gets in
- All alone, looking down on the masses
- Holding onto this pain till more time passes
- And there in between I see through the door... see what needs to be
- And still... you appear so weak to me
- Now monotone sets in and silence fills the air
- Words are better left unspoken.

Stale destiny and the silver moons smile
2002

- Disappearing into a blank mind-expressionless- emotionless
- Hollow background art of faded memories drag me in guilt
- As the ink disappears from the paper on which I write
- Your picture fades
- The reality of all that has been perceived as intruding thoughts-coldy stares you in the face- you are forced into the now
- On the other side of silver moons created long ago, Past sorrows overlooked, beauty stares into my eyes and with that I grip tightly-holding on without taking a moment for granted
- A weighted down form with such intense feelings inside
- Things so real feel like such a dream- a dream I'm dreaming in this life of dreams... I pray I never wake.

Weight of the world

2003

- With shaky hands, like limbs in a storm, I bend and sway but never break
- Soaked in solitude- lonliness gripping me tighter
- I am the non- existent mirage in your life
- I am the over heard whisper
- I am the solution to nothing and the cause of all that fails
- And I am never enough... yet I am the mediator
- I am the center piece
- With this weight on my shoulders, I continue to go on... pushing myself
- Waiting to break. But I won't.

MakeShifT

2003

- These are the words I use/ these are the voices I hear/ these are the feelings

- I continue to strangle/ now I manage to mangle/ these words that I use/

- I do it because the voices tell me to

- Now I strangle myself to end it all/ can't seem to make myself get up when I fall

- Tragically becoming the monster inside

- All of the good that lived in me has died

- Trying to level this field that I play

- So many distractions that get in my way

- I'm stuck in this hole- I thought to be loving

- The image before me is completely disgusting

- In this location, pretending to be

- something I'm not- so it suffocates me
- There is no beginning or end that I can find
- Can't take all this pressure- I'm losing my mind
- Standing on edge- so desperately waiting
- Thinking of jumping- can't stop debating
- Would this all be better, would it all go away?
- If I throw it all out- put myself on display
- Walls closing in, there's no place to run
- I break down as my life comes undone
- Never before have I asked for your help
- But now I stand begging0 there's nobody else
- I'm sinking under. Will you pull me up?

Unborn2

2003

- I want to shed these scars that I hold
- I want to forget tragedies I'm told
- A familiar feeling sets in- oh so deep
- The things that torture me when I sleep
- Another piece of my heart- taken away
- When I received the news today
- I am just trying to be a father
- But why do I even bother?
- Every time we think we're getting close
- We get pain in a larger dose
- I can't help but feel like life's not fair
- Makes me feel like no one cares
- Now I disappear and shed these lonely tears
- Once again eaten alive by my fears
- My child has tried so hard to come into this world

- But every time she does, her life begins to unfurl

- My anger grows so quickly inside me

- It's like some things in life are just not meant to be

- For months the unborn has been my heart

- For a second time, I begin to fall apart

- All at once, her mothers tears fall rapidly

- No one will ever be able to make us see

- Why our child has been taken so mercilessly

The Summary
2003

- What becomes of the things I miss?
- How do I deal wit the pain that exists?
- Search for answers that are so hard to find
- Retracing my steps and losing my mind
- My words, so parallel to all your thoughts
- Being alone, no matter the costs
- And why do I choose to be alone?
- And what will I do when all the world is gone?
- Believe in a world that doesn't exist
- Bring into it all the things I've missed
- Try to pretend everything's ok?
- Try not to think of reality today
- I'm only ever alone on the inside
- I remember the time all the walls cried
- In a reality's dream I was torn apart

- Torn by the nightmare in this lonely heart
- What do you do when your motivation fades away?
- And the skin of a new day rips in dismay?
- Dragging my feet, feeling a bit disconnected
- I begin to crumble as my thoughts are rejected
- I travel the miles in my mind
- Saving a place for all I've left behind
- As I grind my teeth. It echoes in my head
- When I abandon myself, my dreams are dead
- As the streets of thought become empty, I break away from this distraction
- Hiding behind my sturdy wall- in fear of my own reaction
- I hear a voice coming from within-
- clutching my abstract mind- insecurity sets in

- here in a lonely moment, the dragon is branded with his own little number
- under the surface of life- he is pulled under
- my mind seems impervious at any attempt to reconcile
- and my own iniquities shame me all the while
- from here to there go my words of thought
- nothing accomplished, but a lesson taught
- and here it ends- a bunch of ridiculous nonsense
- with the weight of the world riding on my conscience
- as I still struggle to smile and keep the pain inside
- holding onto that part of me that already died
- I lock the key inside and hide behind the wall
- From my metaphorical throne, I pray I never fall

- But I know I will, and that part is scary

- Into the great divine alone I go; with me, my pain I carry

- On my shoulders- and it kills me in the end

- For now I bare scars that time won't mend.

Caving in

2002

- I blame it all on my messed up excuses

- Strangled to death by metaphorical nooses

- Solid white- hard and hollow

- My thoughts- sometimes difficult to follow

- Somewhat tragic and hard to understand

- Holding my heart in the palm of my hand

- Somewhat unstable and full of guilt

- Like the cardboard foundation on which my sanity was built

- Tangled are the thoughts webbed in my head

- It's hard to go on breathing when you're already dead

- And here you are- in my heart

- This is who I am when we are apart

- Only on the inside- the outside you can't see
- The routine of life- taken on by only me
- With something to look forward to, I force myself to go on
- I smile at the thought of another Saturday dawn
- When you are here, everything is bliss
- But during those empty days it's you I miss
- The fact that I am two always comes into play
- But hidden in the shadows is where he will always stay
- You intensify the better part of me
- And when I look in your eyes I love what I see
- All the love you have for me I also have for you
- You keep me from caving in- under skies of dusty blue.

I'm the Reasons

2002

- Disappear- slip in my thought/ dripping with guilt/ I lost it all in one second of a minute I let pass by/ surrounded by everything I pretended not to see/ into my dark place where my body is useless/ here I sit holding my hand/ walking myself/ leading myself to the end to introduce me to myself/ pieces of my life lay crumbled at my feet/ tattered/ shattered/ broken/ torn/ tormented/ twisted/ left alone/ all alone/ peering out my looking glass hoping to catch a glimpse of the hope in something new- that I tell myself pessimistically doesn't exist/ about like me when I sit alone/ swirling thoughts being swallowed by a mouth that doesn't exist/ I see my reflection but can't believe I'm here/ but I continue to see you and you and you and so on and so forth until I don't believe in anything because none of you were ever really there/ haha I say to myself/ haha because once again failure swallowed me.

The Land of No Answers

2002

- Your feelings won't separate themselves

- So if you stare into the sky in search of your answers you go through life gathering riddles that cannot be solved

- I spent a big part of my life searching everywhere for my answers- when all along they were buried within me

- I shove myself into another day, only a fragment of what I used to be

- Leaving pieces of le to those of you who pulled hard enough

- And at times I feel empty- a vast wasteland of useless thought

- At times no one can touch me

- Most often things are grey and blurry- and I'm searching- not for an answer-

- But something...

- Today is one of those days.

1986- From Then On

2003

- Everything inside me begins to turn and flip

- I feel like I'm losing it, so I tighten my grip

- I try to hold on to the world spinning beneath me

- Trying to get out these feelings within me

- I sit... and try to contemplate a decision

- Feeling my way through a dark and confined position

- On the outside I smile while I scream within

- So much pain, where do I begin?

- My first memories as a happy little kid

- I smile as I recall all the things that I did

- But life always throws you a curve

- And we all suffered a loss that we didn't deserve

- Suddenly she's gone and we can't get her back

- Somehow I let hate replace all that I lacked

- Then time continued to tick and things just weren't the same

- In our own ways, we all learned to deal with the pain

- And it's just not fair when you lose your heart

- I stand here today a man torn apart

- Pain has eaten away all the things I kept inside

- On that day, I feel, there was a part of me that died

- Still, I shed not one tear in front of my mothers closed eyes

- But inside I know, she could hear my cries

- And to this day, I know, she still hears those cries

- As I struggle to be the man I know I am inside
- And everyone thinks that I just don't care
- It's the pain that causes the blankness in my stare
- I do the things I do everyday, just to stay alive
- I cannot continue to struggle with the pain I hold inside
- But I'm not going to show it- I won't let it bleed through
- I'm trying to devote and live my life for you
- My wife, so sweet and loving- and I try to show I care
- That's why I leave little notes that say "I love you" everywhere
- And I'm doing the best I can, trying to keep things in order
- Preparing our lives for our son or our daughter
- I wish things were easier, I wish they were better

- But sometimes I feel I could be no deader

- And now I reflect... on my loss and my pain

- Inside my head- hearing my mothers name

- I miss her... and I wish she were here

- To explain everything, make it all seem clear

- What's my purpose? Why am I alive?

- How do I face the man in the mirror mom?

- I wish you could be here when your grandchild comes into this world

- I wish I could touch your face...

- Life is not forever...

All Because of you

2004

- With all our wicked winters buried in the past
- And all our shallow thoughts... and the shadows that they cast
- Drawn into the sun by stars that rule the night
- We mindlessly draw closer- blinded by the light
- Submerged in our faith- we slowly struggle on
- I still taste the tears... long after they're gone
- And bittersweet memories- buried in my past
- Holding tight to blissful emotion- not expecting it to last
- An uneventful stage act this film has turned in to
- Losing my grip on reality... all because of you

Daddys Little Girl

2003

- My heart explodes- the pain runs so deep
- My little girl is gone... and I feel so alone
- This time I can't stop the tears
- I just want her back in my arms
- I fail to understand his plan
- But I can't wait to meet her again
- This world brings me down
- I raise my chin and beg for strength
- As I walk between the valleys under the sky
- Hold my hand... guide me
- Help me heal these wounds
- Daddys little girl- so beautiful... and I love her so much
- I know she's looking down on me
- This pain is much too real
- I said good bye as I held you inmy arms
- Until we meet again, I love you faith

Missing my little girl

2003

- I can think of nothing but the day I hold my little girl again

- She was ripped from my life, but stays in my heart

- I held your little hand and touched your cheek

- I know there is no escape from the pain I feel

- As my journey back to you begins, I feel as though time stands still

- One day, I know, we will meet again- I long to share the love I have inside

- All the things your life could have been

- For now, to heaven, my love I send

- My heart aches as I miss you so

- Faith- I love you more than you'll ever know

The Miracles of Silver Linings
2004

- In the silver linings of shadows under my pale moons gleam

- My emptiness sits alone in the realm of nonexistent illusions

- I woke up and dreamt... to dream of a life, and in a life, live dreams

- The infatuation with it becomes a disease... dead weight, pulling and tugging you under

- There is some relief in giving up- but that is forbidden

- Such a brightly lit sky- beautiful blue- makes me miss the gloomy grey friend that consoles me as I sit my cup of coffee

- As the days come grey, I look to the sky- trying to part clouds for a glimpse of blue, lit by the sun

- Silver linings exist always... although they're often taken for a shade of shiny grey

- The night stars appear cold- many in number- but none the less, alone

- I often relate to stars

- I long to be engulfed by knowledge. I strive, yet the world offers such distractions

- The time is always the same on my clock

- My name written in the dust on the cover of my story

- We've been given wonderful views of existing miracles- the silver linings we take for granted

- When will we open our eyes, come to life... and take in the miracles of blue and grays?

Faith

2003

- Your daddy is trying hard to fight through the pain

- Nothing has hurt this bad in so long

- It's hard to stop the tears from falling

- I know my mom is holding you now

- And that brings a bit of a smile to my face

- My little girl in heaven- you will always be in my heart

- You'll never have to feel our pain, sweetheart

- Even though it hurts so much inside... I know Gods plan for you differed from mine

- I know everything happens for a reason... and I know I will never be able to understand why

- But as you look down me everyday... just know this, my little faith- your daddy loves you

9 Seconds

2003

- Edges frayed and grinding zippers
- Like one big happy trip
- Swirling colors and fighting my own existence
- Tick tocking clock and a million misplaced memories
- The sound only gets louder with time

Change my Direction

2003

- I lend my pain to the reaper of sorrows
- Try to hide from another days tomorrows
- Cloaked in darkness and covered in sin
- Hiding the pain I'm drowning within
- Forcing myself through another day
- Afraid of myself in every single way
- Knowing I'm better off on my own
- Yet, growing restless of being alone
- It moves at night and in the shadows
- To the voices in my head, I lose my battles
- I wish I never knew happiness, so I wouldn't realize I'm sad
- I've single handedly destroyed every dream I've had
- The voices in my head keep repeating what you've said

- No explanation for the origin of my hate
- I manage to destroy everything I create
- No need to fake it- it's on my face
- Rapidly breaking down and falling from grace
- Filling my head are paranoia and confusion
- The life I've made is just an illusion
- I don't need you to hold me under water
- I'm drowning myself- so no one else has to bother.

The Death of a Memory

2004

- The wind blows under gloomy skies, bringing with it the smell of rain
- Something in the back of mind is burning- I faintly smell the smoke from the flames
- Maybe an old memory- something I want forgotten
- Perhaps something useless, boxed up, collecting dust on the shelves in my head
- The wind calms... only for a second... a second long enough to hear the crackling of fire- to know that something is beginning to fade
- I suppose I will never realize what it was, or what replaced it...but a part of me is gone with it I'm sure
- Another step towards the end
- Oh my sweet memory- defenseless in my head- I'm sorry you were forgotten.

Twisted Symphony

2004

- Down this unenchanted road I go...
  bouncing of the torturing stones...
  climbing mountains made of glass...
  nothing I do ever seems to last

- So I close my eyes and scream aloud

- Trying to force the words from my
  mouth

- Trying to understand the things I do

- Wondering why I take this from you

- Lying down with my ear to the
  ground, "you're closer now", I
  whisper to the sound

- And the winds swirl as I lose my grip

- Sooner or later I was bound to slip

- The trees that hang over this road

- Tempt me silently with every word

- I am a contradiction as I grit my teeth

- But no one sees what lies beneath

- Under this mold I wear everyday

- You will see when the skin fades away
- When the trees fall and the clouds begin to cry
- Like tiny daggers falling from the sky
- Then my tongue unravels and the truth comes out
- Everything that plagues me is caused by doubt
- By someone or something... or maybe it's you
- No one is responsible for the things you do
- Now, in my mind your words become twine
- Forming a noose in the back of my mind
- Maybe you'll use it at my weakest time
- Maybe you won't... I really don't mind
- Spirals still swirl- blankets still cover
- I am not the one...and there is no other.

Prone to Drown

2004

- It breaks away, ever so swiftly
- Connecting with another and beginning immensely
- Dragging the bottom of the lake for clues
- An unhesitant response leaves nothing but a bruise
- To remind you that you were here and you almost drown
- Cut by the edge and faded by the sound
- A brightly lit sun scorches the skin
- As one dies, another begins
- Disrupted thoughts take their revenge
- To grip the throat of action and begin to avenge
- To render you useless in your translucent cage
- Sink deeper into your mind- then turn the page

- It's always blank, like the expression on your face
- Look into the mirror and stare at a waste
- Compulsive to the point that this has to end
- Surrounded by walls that are much too thin
- And one little hand can set you free
- But your actions are binded by the thoughts in me
- So one more time I tear myself down
- I thought I was swimming... but I've already drown.

Burned by the Sun

2003

- Decisions of few, with little left to view

- I live my life with you- to the point when I'm through

- When I'm dead and gone

- And my spirit carries on

- To place to place- I don't know

- But so badly, I long to go

- To hold my Faith and smile

- And forget for a little while

- That I ever lost her at all

- How will I know when the time is right?

- When the blocks don't fit because the corners are too tight

- And my decorated life- like lights for this world

- Will never replace my precious baby girl

- Now I have this pain

- As I scream your name
- And there's nothing you can say
- That can take this pain away
- Nothing can be done
- As I'm burned by the sun
- On the edge of the earth
- Where we lost her at birth
- The tears still fall- I'm sick of it all
- When the last page has its turn- my name you will learn.

Rerun Star

2004

- A rounded corner- smooth but jagged
- Tormenting myself until I've had it
- The film stops and begins to shred
- The movie ends because the star is dead
- One more loss we caught on tape
- How much more can one heart take?
- and where does it end? I have to know
- How much further can one heart go?
- I tend to struggle as life gets in the way
- It cages my emotions and the words I should say
- Living in reruns my life is less than fun
- But I knew I was finished when the movie was done.

Shatter

2005

- I only see that face when it rains
- Only when it drowns me in my pain
- Only when I face the reality in me
- Running from the hatred that I feel and see
- Only grey above and a chilling cold
- I don't seem to fits my lifes mold
- A little out of place and out of my mind
- My bringer of sorrows has never been kind

- Close your eyes one more time. Feel it inside one more time. Only words that mean nothing. Only feelings that don't matter. Only the dreams I'll eventually shatter.

- Over and over, thread by thread...
- I unravel life until the story is dead

- The skin dries up and the wind takes it away
- As I kick my teeth in everyday
- Alone I shatter, in all my guilt
- And remain lost in the maze I've built

I See Me (In the eyes of the enemy)
2005

- In the mirror I stand again
- Face to face with the monster that is becoming my end
- Whenever that may be
- Staying afloat in a struggle, just trying to be me
- But then again I wonder who he really is
- The one who studies my eyes as I study his
- His scars all match the same in every way
- Except inside- they don't feel the same way
- As I look into his eyes, I see nothing inside]
- I try to divide- look away and hide- but there he is with me, stride for stride
- A piece of the puzzle is missing, for he doesn't have a heart

- And the things he puts me through tear mine apart
- So I continue to struggle and mess up my life
- Plunging it in again ... and turning the knife
- Until the pain fades and I have none left to hide
- Until he can't see through me- see what I hold inside.

Untitled 3

2004

- This dreary cold I swallow- and all the pain that follows
- The things I live for- to breath in my mistakes
- The great divine alone- I can't escape the reflection
- All shredded and laid at my feet
- Shards of glass grind in my ear
- A bitter cold that grasps my voice
- There's a direction I should go- but my chains prevent me from making a right turn
- Dimming lights burn me as I follow a dead end
- I keep going until I come to a wall
- Then I lay down, close my eyes... and avoid it all.

Every September

2004

- Every September I feel this way
- Like a broken record that continues to play
- Like a struggling breeze that refuses to blow
- Writing down what I cannot show
- Walking an edge that comes to its end
- Every September it begins again
- Like crackling fire on a burning piece of paper
- We'll all die sooner or later
- I hold my head high and hope for the best
- And forge ahead when put to the test
- Expecting not to see it coming when it does
- He died in September... and that's the way it was
- But I still smile and hope to be free
- From an emotion I let consume me
- And I'll keep fighting so not to remember
- The way I felt every September.

Crooked Smile

2004

- here in the shadows- fears comfort me one by one

- I fall prey to an agonizing struggle for leadership within

- Distant waters crash against a broken shore

- Dead thoughts float face down on the surface

- This waiting pool that I wade through rises to my crooked smile

- You see my tongue through shattered teeth

- Coiled and impaled by silver

- Growing dull with every word

- Speaking truth behind a mask of lies

- End the end, none of it has meant anything

- And somewhere near the middle I stop to think

- As I remember, I catch my second wind... right after I lose my first breath
- I draw back and retrace my steps
- And look once more to the crooked smile in the mirror...
- He has no idea who I am.

Feel Hollow

2005

- How I became what I am today... the answer eludes me constantly

- Those I worry needlessly...

- Words disappear, feelings never exist...

- Or maybe they're so abundant that they blend with the pain?

- I keep trying- finding stones to cast at my reflection

- Mirror man feels no pain

- I once feared him, no long to be him- or anyone else

- Tangled in my own web- I create the chaos in my head

- I feel intense... about what?

- I forgot to remember what I swore I'd never do...

- Do what the moments urge me to..

- A lonely walk or heavy breathing don't change minds

- A walking brick wall... you can't hurt me anymore
- I'll take the pain you bring- watch me smile
- You're lost and you don't know me anymore
- I belong to the heart of the lonely and broken
- I am the thunder over head- and rain calms me
- I'm not alone... everyone feels the way I do
- And now the truth surfaces again... I will never know him... I will never feel
- I hate myself today ... and in the midst of self frustration
- I hear a voice calling my name

Why Must I Feel this Way
2005

- A little blurry and hard to see
- The pain you feel lives in me
- A cracked reflection of the person I wanted to be
- Growing angrier with the man I see
- Deep inside where my true feelings lie
- With all the past iv'e shoved inside
- A nervous smile and a silent prayer
- Never letting go of my mirror image stare
- A twisted symphony of pain and regret
- With little sprinkles of bliss- hasn't killed me yet
- And now another shoulder to lean on and break
- To take another step... and learn from another mistake.

Untitled 4

2005

- The looks I give with the face I wear
- Through the mask, into the mirror I stare
- Face to face I stand with madness
- Every bit of me consumed by sadness
- All the pieces of my life are broken
- With every single word that's spoken
- Between splitting thought I bury my lie
- Unable to escape the monster inside
- No matter the effort in the try
- Deep inside I shed my fear- wear it in the form of a smile
- Every single step into a broken mile.

Rise

2003

- When I look up at this day... feeling scarred and feeling blamed
- Everything I hold inside- everything locked inside my mind
- Feels its chance to come alive and find my way back to my life
- I feel such hatred inside
- I get so lost in my find
- You've lost yourself for the last time
- I see my future in your eyes
- Brush away the feelings like I don't care
- Kiss away sorrow when life's not fair
- Lick the wound that keeps me bleeding
- Find the center of what I'm needing
- Erase the mistakes that I've made
- And gently, slowly... begin to fade.

Dirty Thought

2003

- one little dirty thought you never heard

- in the back of your mouth where you choked on your words

- one little scar that will not heal

- across your heart- and bleeds what you feel

- this isn't really what makes you sad... this isn't what makes you cry

- it's always the past that brings you down

- in your shattered dreams and all too vivid memories- your scars still hurt

- one little dirty thought you refuse to hear

- in the back of your mind where you hide from your fear

- this isn't real... tell yourself... this isn't real... keep saying it

- it never will be.

Content

2003

- Proceed with such limitations... deliverance comes within a blue moons eye

- Trickling tears and the fairytales our former inner child believed

- Sleepless in a dream- nightmare in pursuit

- Vivid hallucinations of purity you never had

- Mouths sewn shut by invisible twine

- Another wasted thought- an idea that was never spewed from a mouth

- So much over dramatic nonsense... packaged up like important somethings

- All in one moment everything you can't understand becomes clear...

- Then you're content.

I Wasn't Ready
2004

Marks made on bitter hearts dry the lonely tears inside

- Scratching the surrounding white walls- removing the skin from bone

- A dreary rain on an October evening

- Nothing but fond memories murdered by sorrow

- Black skies swallow me as I look into forever

- I wasn't ready for this.

- Cold skin.

- I am broken and empty

- October shows no mercy

- And I have no emotions left to destroy.

Writers Block

2004

- Tell them again and the sound carries into the back of my mind

- Drifting away into frayed thought- the shame swept under the rug

- I begin to shed layers odd misconception and hate

- Falling back into a mask of skin- a charred feeling of familiarity

- A cataclysmic shock of truth… the undertow of my life still pulling me down

- I'm setting my feet firmly and holding onto fragile limbs

- Here is the struggle… a little hill to overcome

- A blackout of misunderstood proportions

- Always feels more tragic than it really is

- It only lasts a little while.

Shackles of the Mind

2005

- Breathe in the sadness and hold tight your grip... on the edge of darkness that lies on the tip of your tongue...emerging like jagged daggers... unsturdy pieces... unsturdy and on the verge of broken

- Sanity is so fragile... dipped in fear and sprinkled with remorse... filed away in the minds of what we were moments ago

- Merely the glare of lonely stars awakens the breathless from a jaded slumber

- Open eyes spy the outline of failure... an unconceivable design for life... and very comical if you view the way I do

- Life has the irony to match every emotion- most of which I lack... just a broken shard of glass lodged beneath the skin... scraping the bone... like an interruption of silence

- When seconds seem like forever the puzzle is incomplete... emptiness is a descendant of the sadness that swirls around you... binds your thoughts... a barricade for blissful thoughts
- I see through the cracks... I know how to the open door
- But I remain silent with my feet shackled to the floor.

3 Pages
2005

- Three pages until I resurface again... until I bend- then break... split open and drug through the mud again
- Through the wet cold of a twisted mind... fenced in- yet unable to contain
- Tiny lines through my vision... blood collecting at my feet
- Light playing the opposing role to shadows
- One giant shadow of the mind- a darkness in my head
- Only rain can calm a contorting force of violence
- Peeling away the false layers of pretending to finally see the face of my enemy
- Three pages until the dust settles and we see who is left... left standing... left waiting... left alone... and prove wrong.

Self- Destructive Reflection

2005

- Self destructive patterns forming over icy blue stares

- Holding on to my pretentious hope when it was never really there

- All my emotion showing- I can't control the pain

- Not knowing what I know now- the silence drives me insane

- Equal to that which I see

- Pain can cripple a broken heart- everything I live through consumes all of me

- I can't breath as I once did- the stiffness in my lungs settles in

- As I face the torment in the mirror- knowing it's a battle I'll never win

- I died tonight- and all my walls came down

- Filter out my pain- and get lost in my sound

Too Deep

2005

- I'm out of breath- this world is suffocating

- Losing my thoughts now- in a mind that there is no saving

- I blame my failure on the hatefulness inside

- I close my eyes now- and in my head I hide

- My eagerness to destroy me is overcome by fear

- Uncomfortable in my skin, my path has become clear

- This self destruction of all that I've become

- A physiological thriller- where all my achievements come undone

- And nightmares under my bed come to life and strangle me in my sleep

- I'd like to hold your hand and lead you
  in… but the blood is much too deep

Stationary Smile

2005

- Every sentence- every sin
- Every blade drug across my skin
- Every hour of my days I live in dismay
- Wasted moments washed away
- Like a prison cell for every time I fail
- Every crack you peer through
- The distance from me to you
- The simplicity of unbelievable truth
- Sitting alone in the sublime comfort of dark
- Contemplating when to make my mark
- Following the trail of blood to the mirror
- Closing my eyes to see the image clearer
- Face to face... lost in disarray
- Confused for a moment- then able to break away
- I begin to drift and lose my grip
- And bury myself under all I've built

To my son and daughter
2005

- You'll be here soon and I'll hold you in my arms

- Protect your world and keep you from harm

- I await the day when my sanity will arrive

- To keep me from growing so cold inside

- My daughter- my Faith- always in my heart

- I carry you with me- we are never apart

- I pray for perfection in the birth of my son

- But always know- you were the one

- The one who first touched my heart and made all this real

- Nothing can change the way I feel

- Your little brother will soon be here

- I embrace his arrival- I have no fear

- I'm ready to be the father I didn't get to be to you
- I feel my emotions beginning to shine through
- A new chapter of my life- as you watch over us with care
- And nothing can change the bond we share
- Father and daughter- a love so true
- Always know, that's how I feel about you
- To my son, I say this:
- Your dad will greet you with a kiss
- And know I'll love you all your life

- It's why I'm here... I know that now.

Can't Breathe

2006

- There's a place in my head where I try to go
- To escape a world I don't want to know
- Because in this place you can't save them all
- Boiled emotions- inside, tears fall
- The reflection has faded but his laugh I can still hear
- From beyond the grave- still force feeding fear
- I won't hear these echoes of pain
- With broken thoughts driving me insane
- You can't save them all- as I see him wasting away
- As the pain repeats its role in this part I play
- I wish you were here to save us from this

- Holding your grandson in sublime bliss
- But life's not fair- so you're not here
- Taking your place here is my own fear
- I feel like I can't do this anymore
- Dragging my mind across my hearts floor
- Even in an empty mirror, I still can't forget
- Or ignore all my own regret
- I wish I could do so much more
- It's my wife and son I would do it for
- And my moments are blessed with the two of them here
- The time of action has to be near
- My inner fight- I feel I've won
- And the world around me fails to understand what I've done
- I feel like these words hold no release
- No freedom at all- the pain doesn't cease
- I'm holding onto what I've got
- Close my eyes and pray to lose it not

- Release- and calm… and lay down your head
- Everything will be better tomorrow, I said
- Stay away from the dark place in the back of your mind
- Do that- and you'll be just fine

Eyes of my Child

2006

- A dark cloud lifts as the emptiness I've always felt disappears
- That something that I've searched for has poured into my heart and changed my life
- A love like no other, as I stare into my sons eyes
- The most intense feeling I've ever felt
- Coming from a place deeper than I knew my heart went
- There is nothing I wouldn't do to protect this child of mine
- His life is more important than anything to me
- My love for him overcomes and becomes me
- In his innocent eyes I see so much
- So much of me I see in him
- This little man has my heart- now and forever
- Locked away behind his beautiful eyes

About Face

2006

- The mistakes I've made have torn me apart
- The lies I've lived have broken your heart
- But I won't be beaten by the face in the mirror
- The path I seek has become much clearer
- Here and now I vow to be-
- The man inside you deserve me to be
- To provide, protect and give you all of me
- I long to be a man I would want my son to be
- The rapid decease of this structure fire
- I never wanted to be a liar
- I only want to take care of you
- Here and now- I say I do
- To remain true for the rest of our days
- Feeling alive coming out of this haze

- As for the darkness that has lived in my mind
- I long to start over and leave it behind
- The man I was is no longer here
- For the rest of our lives- you have nothing to fear
- I can be the light at the end of the tunnel for you
- Believe in love and I will see you through
- I believe in our family and I believe this to be true:
- I am still the man that is madly in love with you.

13
2005

- 13 eyes with 13 smiles
- 13 ways to drive you wild
- 13 ways to find your mate
- 13 ways you'll learn to hate
- 13 ways to lay down and die
- 13 faces with 13 smiles
- 13 lessons taught in the night
- 13 times you've lost the fight
- 13 emotions that I hide inside
- From the 13 personalities that I divide.

13 Eyes

2006

- Behind the mirror lies the face

- corrosion begins and sets in place

- Starring into my eyes, I make my heart race

- And steal away my smile without a trace

- There is a hesitation- then there's a pause

- Stare at the reflection and lose the cause

- It's really irrelevant when you consider the crime

- But no opposing thoughts were presented at the time

- The 13 smiles behind these eyes

- Have become tangled and hung in my web of lies.

Desire You

2006

- I haven't a clue how I brought me to this

- Facing emotions- desire I can't resist

- Two circles that I get lost inside

- I see more than my reflection in your eyes

- Every kiss leaves me wanting you still

- I barely believe that this is real

- Every glance turns into a stare

- Where ever my thoughts wander- I find you there

- Blissful and frustrating at the same time

- Searching for a way to make you mine

- To dig myself from the hole I'm in

- Here I am- knocked right off my feet again

- I turn around to see the drug that I've been breathing in

- My addiction to you makes it easier to give in
- I forget everything- but it's ok- just kiss me again

My Every Thing

2006

- The English language holds no words to describe the love I hold in my heart for you- angel of my dreams

- Waking to the realization that the dream is real- you are my wife, my love, my friend... everything I searched for so long ago

- Here in my heart this emotion grows strong

- I've deeply loved you for so long

- All I know is that you are my wife

- I long to make you happy for the rest of your life

- You are the one that was meant for me

- Our little family is the way it should be

- To the ends of the earth, your love I would follow

- My soul mate... my mandi... I love you.

Self Desire

2006

- Desire me so deeply- twist and crease my frame
- Clip the frayed edges around the skin
- expose the broken heart within
- Desire me so deeply- so paste me on the wall
- Hang me up with I rusty nail
- Highlight every time I fail
- Desire me so deeply- break my fingers beneath your feet
- Hold me under so I don't breath
- When the bubbles stop, take a moment to grieve
- You desired me so deeply- you brought me to life
- With eyes of glass you starred me down
- I remember the moment you faded... without a sound.

Because of You

2006

- The things I've lost- the things I've gained
- The little things that drive me insane
- The love for my son- the love for my wife
- The ways I've tried to destroy my life
- My other half- I hold so dear
- The only reason I'm still here
- Now I have two- I know I've been blessed
- Thanks to them- the shadow has regressed
- The things I feel- the things I do
- Nothing can deny my love for you
- Finally escaping the past- and starting over new
- My life would have been pointless without you
- These things I say- I really feel
- My emotions for you are genuinely real

- How I love you so…
- I'm forever yours- this you must know
- You and I will grow old together
- Sharing a soul mate bond forever
- Watch over our son- grow and love
- And be thankful for our blessings from above.

The Defeated Reflection

2006

- You thought you had me- and you came so close

- Now you are nothing- only a ghost

- Fading into the shadows to be forgotten

- The grip you lost is the grasp I've gotten

- I stand facing this shattered reflection

- It is you who now seeks protection

- You are defeated as you face your foe

- The love for my son has broken you- this you must know

- It's all in your head that you really exist

- It's completely irrelevant that you try and resist

- I've won the battle as you disappear

- I've finally conquered my greatest fear

- The fear was me- coiled in anger and pain

- The war was pointless before Tyler came
- Emptiness fades as I look into my sons face
- It all ends here and now- and in this place
- In my head where I'll strike you down
- And in all the pain you've caused... I'll let you drown.

Ramblings of Half a Man
2006

- Mid September- grey and gloomy
- My sons eyes watch everything curiously
- He smiles at me and melts my heart
- The world outside of ours is different
- Unhappy- unchanged, and a bit dreary
- Cold rain urges my purpose
- My other half is unaccounted for
- I almost feel empty
- I feel a single drop of rain... then another
- As if someone hears my thoughts and grants my wishes
- I wish that were true
- I wish to be at a point in the future-
- Skipping the time between then and now- then again I don't
- I want to cherish every moment in between
- Sometimes I get lost in my tangled thoughts
- I feel like this is one of those moments

The Path

2006

- Around the corners and down the side
- Bleeding a path to what's inside
- Smoke-screen- blinded, and drenched from the rain
- Breaking the skin- clearing a path for pain
- I hide from myself in the midst of glory
- Telling myself lies to build my story
- Light shines through an open wound
- I hope my answers will be coming soon
- In the meantime- my time I will bide
- Searching for the darkest corner- so I can hide.

Lost My Way

2006

- He stands and shouts, "I killed me"
- He stands and shouts, "can't you see?"
- He lays down and slowly bleeds
- What did I do to deserve to be me?
- He bows his head and says "goodbye"
- Tonight's the night my feelings die
- He lets go and says, "I've really lost my way"
- He grasps what he has- " I won't let this go away"
- "I will not fail anymore"- as he closes the door
- Now I open my eyes as my lonely heart dies
- I've never seen this before
- My grip's not tight anymore
- " I've lost my way"
- I need your guiding hand
- I want to be this man that hides inside
- Now my heart breaks... I won't let love die... help me save it.

Untitled 5

2006

- With a love so deep it could drown the seas, I open up my heart
- Your home forever, as it has been from the start
- With one glance- my breath- you take away
- I thank heaven for you, each and everyday
- The silver moon compares nothing to thee
- I'm so lucky you fell in love with me
- Only God knows why you've stuck with me so long
- And loved me unconditionally, no matter what I've done wrong
- And that love, in return, I plan on giving to you
- Until our dying day, may my love remain true

- To find your soul mate is something rare
- I look forward to the life ahead that we'll share
- I love you with a passion that burns so deep
- You as my wife- forever- I intend to keep
- Being so much more than just a wife
- You're the best friend I've known all my life
- In my mind, I see us grow old
- Ours is the greatest story never told
- And now we are forever chained to the bliss of being in love with one another.

A Tyler Type of Feeling

2006

- Here's a feeling I've never gotten
- All my pain has been forgotten
- I wonder how I dealt before
- I won't feel that way anymore
- It feels like a battle has just been won
- I owe it all to my precious son
- A little version of me- so weak and small
- I feel no emptiness inside at all
- Just one smile to make me cry
- What power possessed by a tiny little guy
- I'll love him forever, but I always remember
- The way I felt that day in December
- The same way I feel now
- I can't help but wonder how
- Someone so small could own my heart
- I know I've found my missing part

Cold Thinking (sharing thoughts)
2007

Anybody ever notice that cold weather changes you? Makes you a little different as a person? Well, it has an effect on me anyway. What is it specifically about the cold... there must be a scientific explanation for what happens when the weather gets colder. I begin to think a lot more. Not to say I never think... it tends to make me reflect. I find myself becoming a very odd person in cold. (if me being more odd is possible) It brings about a lot of different feelings. A lot of flashbacks... regret...a little sadness... rained on by all my happy moments. Makes me resent things I have no control over. I wish for a lot of things. That life was simpler... that I could see my family whenever I wanted... that I had more time to do all the little things (but I suppose more time would only mean more thinking)

Wish I really believed everything happens for a reason when I say it. Wish I could take away the pain of loved ones. Wish I wasn't so depended on by everyone I work with.

Wish only those I want to could see me. Sometimes I wish the weather would stay this way because it makes me comfortable in my own skin for a change. Wish I got to choose the days it would rain. Wish every radio station (no matter the genre) played the cure. Wish I didn't try to fix everything that's broken... (some things should just stay broken) wish television channels still played music videos... good ones....but besides all that, don't take me the wrong way. I am a happy person. I haven't always been... it's nice. I'm just a little strange... no, I'm misunderstood a lot. I wish everyone got to know the real me... but the fact that they don't might be a good thing. But right now it's cold. Not too cold. A little windy...it's dark. It's ok. I like it. And there is an odd, familiar feeling in the air. Makes you want to sit back and really think about things. Maybe it's just me, but I don't think so. Wish I had more time to read and write. I enjoy that most. Life is pretty short... I mean, years aren't as long as you might think. Days go by rather quickly. You won't get everything on your list done. Pick what's most important I guess. Take care of that, it will have to suffice. Wish I didn't have the tendency to go on babbling in such padded walls fashion. But I'm only being Mickey.

The Day it Rained

2007

- The rain falls swiftly; like my feelings reincarnated
- The distant rumble keeps my mind aware of the world around me
- My skin cold; yet warm to the touch
- Like a premonition... a nostalgic feeling engulfs every bit of me
- A lucid mind kept company by the storm
- At peace within the intensity of its chaos
- One day it rained... then it poured
- In the midst, brewed my storm...
- Dark and windy, full of pain... noosed in silver...pushing the tear soaked trees back and forth...
- The thunder spoke to me in ways so familiar
- The fear that it would soon pass- widespread in my mind
- The day it rained... I prayed it would last forever.

Diamonds in the Rough

2007

- I wolf in sheeps clothing, but only to myself
- Close my eyes, grit my teeth- and slowly lose my breath
- My level of function is- I can't get out of bed
- Lack of motivation- due to the darkness in my head
- Now it's dark… only for a moment
- Grasping love, and thankful to own it
- Hold it and twist my vines around her heart
- Feelings so intense- they rip me apart
- Torn and shredded… at my own feet I lay
- Disregarding myself in my own vicious way
- Never letting go- my two diamonds in the rough

- Only factors that hold me up in this life so tough
- I am a wall- you'll never make me fall
- In crippled fashion- I give in to it all

Stalked

2007

- The 13th of Friday, and black is the night
- The rain falls swiftly with one star in sight
- I wish I may; you wish I might
- Spare you my head trip for one more night
- Just step in my shadow and share my smile
- Listen closely, you may be here awhile
- Close your eyes and listen to the sound
- Of my foot steps moving the leaves on the ground
- As I follow you closely, you become nervously aware
- Your heart beats quicker, for you know that I am there
- Quicken your step and focus; the destination

- Your thoughts may wander to ideas of devastation
- Choking on your fear, you wonder if I'm gone
- Truth be told- I was within you all along

The Imaginary Monster
Who Took the Blame

2007

- Edit my view and help me set things right
- Previous battles have left me too weary to fight
- The way I perceive is assisted by my mind
- Now owning the feelings I have sought to find
- Continuing to fall in love everyday
- Making my heart a slave, in her own special way
- Looking so proudly into the eyes of my son
- Being the greatest thing that I've ever done
- Loving them two- more than my own soul
- Giving me life- making me whole
- So edit my view but the feelings remain
- The reflection in the mirror isn't the same
- The monster has gone- replaced with a smile
- Self loathing no longer my style
- Starring back is a husband and a father
- Leaving the past behind even farther
- Losing myself in the blackness of the night

- Blinded by the sun, yet never losing sight
- Fistful of regret; wrapped in an optimistic grin
- Playing a game I'm destined to win
- Just in my reach- happiness sat still
- I grasped and held tight with all my will
- In the end- after I'm gone
- Please forgive me of all my wrongs
- And follow the road that leads you home
- Resting in my arms, where you belong
- Freedom found from a violent stare
- But the question remains- was he ever really there?

Dark veil of the 13th Reason

2007

- A dark veil is lifted- the sun burns uncontrollably through the tear

- New illusions appear- seeing through the fantasies, I wander suspiciously

- Expecting the world to break in two... divide reality from my mind

- The day passes without break... the curtain closes

- The dark veil once again blankets out eyes

- Brightly lit- piercing diamonds stare back at us

- Daring us to speak the truth... the clock moves quickly in the night

- The veil lifts once again... I continue to search for proof of this false reality

- The crescent moon smiles... it smirks at the fact that I am it's puppet

- It tugs on my strings... dangling just out of reach of safety

- Injecting me with the insanity that I live with
- Suddenly we are once again blind folded
- Sinker deeper into my skin... I realize... all we have to do is open our eyes
- Open our eyes and peer into the night... in search of truth
- The 13th reason I fight with my mind- to find the break
- To reveal the lie... to lift the veil one final time.

Love... and the Invincible Reflection

2007

- My panic prone, grief stricken, beautiful inside out way of staring into a mirror and creating a make believe monster out of a single glance reflects on my lack of strength to be who I am

- Afraid of myself- pretending to battle a reflection to justify my confusion

- Life is as we see it through our everyday eyes- without urgent smiles and slippery hands... silver tongues that tell our stories

- Mine began with jagged edges and was worn smooth by love

- Imprisoning my heart in a cage of bliss... dredging my soul for strength and dragging my tired feet across lifes floor

- Thank God for my wife and son... my here- on- earth defenders

- I love you both uncontrollably.

Here I Stand

2008

- Here I stand, made of steel
- Here I stand, my wickedness shown
- Here I stand, drenched in pain
- Here I stand, feeling betrayed
- Here I stand, confused and lost
- Here I stand, fighting anger
- Here I stand, I loves reach
- Here I stand, not letting go
- Here I stand, seeking strength
- Here I stand, unable to think straight
- Here I stand, holding back tears
- Here I stand- here I stand

- Loving you still… understanding
- Trying to look past the pain that's killing me
- The thoughts I don't want to have…the emotions I want to escape
- Unable to believe truth… it's you

- Still can't believe... but I'm trying
- Here I stand, outstretched hand
- Take it... take it and walk with me
- Walk with me through pain showers
- And see that I am still forever in love with you.

Inches 2 Go

2008

- Only inches to go; grip tight your blade
- Slip into your mask for this masquerade
- Parade around in fashions grotesque
- Save for the wicked what they do best
- Inches to go so drag your blade
- Darkness consumes as light tends to fade
- Admire my smile, for it is hard fought
- Finally attaining the happiness I sought
- Still faced with demons; the voices are still the same
- The thoughts disappear as quickly as they came
- Inches to go, so break the skin
- Ignore the pain that begins to set in
- Everything you ever do is never what it seems
- Uncontrollable emotions finally burst the seams

- The inches to go are in the past as the blade reaches it's end
- Always remember; the reflection is no friend
- He will claw at your heart every chance you give
- So murder the man in the mirror if you want to live

I tend to write everything in metaphor… so it may sound like I'm speaking of physically hurting one's self, when I'm merely suggesting to disregard a thought .. or simply changing my ways…. I'm sure it only makes sense to me.

- M

Beats the same

2008

- My thoughts are closing in; reality is a dream
- The walls are much too thick; I can't hear myself scream
- I hold myself; I'm never letting go
- I feel no pain- as long as I always know
- You're here for me- you mean so much
- I drown in love- electrified by your touch
- People tend to change but my heart beats the same
- It's what you gave- the lost soul you save
- Thank you for love and never giving up
- Your love I take- I'll never get enough
- Slowly slowing down- remembering the sound- now I'm giving in
- To the love I'm living in

- I will never be the same, as I scream your name
- Reality is my dream- my heart beats the same
- I'm never giving up- I'm never letting go
- Onto you I still hold
- A fraction of myself- becoming who you are
- This dream I'm living in is too good... but it's true
- Simple recipe... two soul mates and some prayers
- On tested ground we stand... not phased by the sound
- As the world begins to fade
- Two hearts becoming one... both still beat the same
- Standing in loves rain... let it wash over me
- Cleanse all my regret; never look back as we walk together
- Hand in hand forever

Untitled 6

2008

- Never did I imagine my life as it is today
- Never did I imagine finding my soul mate
- Someone so beautiful- inside and out
- Someone so smart and funny. So caring, so loving
- Someone I couldn't live without
- Like feeling incomplete and finding the other half of myself
- The very thought of you brings about a smile and makes my heart race
- An incredible person that, for some reason, chose to spend the rest of her life with me
- I know I am truly blesses
- I love you more than I can imagine any one loving another
- You are the beat of my heart and the breath in my lungs

- Soul mate says so much... and yet not nearly enough
- The world seems to fade away when our lips meet in a kiss
- I vow to love you with all that I am- for as long as God leaves me on this earth
- The depths of my love is impossible to measure
- To know that the way I feel for you is returned in the same fashion is an overwhelming emotion
- I love you so much... my home is in your heart and our love is forever etched upon mine

Aftermath

2008

- I still hear the laugh, but can't see the face
- Driven under my skin by the sanity of this place
- Always separated, but never letting go
- Ignorant to everything that I'll ever know
- Forced to the ground and bound against my will
- By the thoughts that shackle me- and the anger that I feel
- It disappears and reappears without any notice
- Clouds my mind and twists my focus
- Like looking through the eyes of a perfect stranger
- Walking off the edge- never sensing the danger
- Eager to please and quick to fail

- Torturing myself in my own personal hell
- Losing sight of what is real
- Distracted by the way I feel
- Not taking for granted the gift that is today
- Not hanging on the words that you didn't say
- Feeling it all fade when I look into your eyes
- Heavens eyes under lavender skies
- And all this goes through my head in a second of a thought
- Starring into an empty mirror... remembering battles fought.

Waiting to be Saved

2008

- What to do with this disposable anger
- Shift them around and strangle the stranger
- Strangers are the thoughts that invade my head
- They are not mine- but some one else's instead
- I'm not like this- this isn't who I intended to be
- Waiting patiently for something to save me

Point of me

2008

- What is the point of being me if I cannot see what I am doing?

- What is the point of being free if I cannot feel what I am thinking?

- What is the point of going mad when all that is in store is self destruction?

- The darkness that blankets me lights your way to my broken smile

- Where the person on the outside and the one on the inside struggle to co-exist

- What's the point of all my madness? The world around me moves unaware of my presence

- A tiny speck on the cheek of nothingness... holding on to be seen for a moment... only to be brushed away into oblivion

- What's the point of my words?

- No one is listening.

Untitled 7

2008

- Suffocate me under dark blanket skies
- Twist my fragile image into oblivion
- Rip the tainted smile from my face
- I am a silhouette of nothing; kept in a safe place
- You are the wound upon my flesh
- Repeat my name again and again
- You deserve this.

Dragon Avoid Defeat

2008

- A tangled emotion lost in my head-without help

- How did I get so broken?

- Left with a mountain of words unspoken

- Difficult to think… as I look on and grit my teeth

- My hand always seems just out of reach

- Now… without the faintest of smiles, I sigh

- Tragedies befallen, I still find the strength to try

- Open eyes deny- I still find the moments to cry…captured and bliss stricken- the circle is now complete

- Once again- the lonely dragon has avoided defeat.

Untitled 8

2008

- With a smile twisting around me
- Impervious to the control you have over me
- The rest of my life becoming shorter with each moment
- Moments dampened by the visions
- The visions forming a ring around the flame that burns down my heart
- Boils my blood and shapes the wicked smile painted on my face
- With teary eyes I wave good bye
- Next time will be different... and in that, together we will grow stronger
- Our combined intellect and strength will make us superior to the ones groveling at our feet
- Step inside- close the door behind you
- It's time to wake up.

Hide and Found

2008

- Take what you will/ break away to feel
- Count the seconds until it's time/ look behind these eyes to find
- Find 13 little grins behind these teeth/ locked away, like the feelings beneath
- Hearts wrapped in chain/ set afire by my flame
- Boast and stand confident with clenched fists/ oblivious to all the moments I've missed
- Gave into anger/ unlucky enough to fall in love with the danger
- Taken aside by an alter ego/ laughing in the reflective face of the hero
- Here he sat- right within me all along- making me whole in a sick way/ crafty and cunning- hanging on every word that I say
- Now he creeps out of hiding/ there's no finding/ finding of peace
- I told me so.

Deliver the Cross
2008

- Drift into sorrow and pour myself a drink
- Too tired to care and too sober to think
- Bearing all my pain and carrying it for you
- Designing my own resolution but forgetting what to do
- Caressing my scars to remember who I am
- The man in the mirror still better than I am
- Never measuring up- never getting it right
- But it's been a long war, and I'm too tired to fight
- So lay me down to sleep- I hope and I pray
- At least help me be the best I can every day

- Only a single candle lights my way in the dark
- Only a single candle- one flame burning hot
- Dripping hot tears on my flesh- on my flesh
- Smell of divine death and angels breath
- Heavens lassos turning to nooses – blind eyes open
- The earth twist and contorts beneath my feet
- My mood changes with the wind
- Help me... there is someone or something in my head with me
- Forcing my pen to insanity- gritting my teeth and crawling up my spine
- Up my spine like slippery razor blades
- Crimson tears run down my back
- My red cape making puddles at my feet
- I am still too tired to fight
- My muscles have no use for me
- My mind casts me aside

- Bury me in the wall and hang a pretty picture over my face
- Or open your eyes and see me drowning
- Save me
- Or enjoy the show

Obsession
2008

- Obsession has an ugly face/ it steals away my happy moments

- Learn to let go- give yourself chance

- Life minus the strife

- Obsession has an ugly face

- As you wallow, you bring down your world

- Love suffers, innocence sheds a tear

- Baffled, I stand, unable to comprehend

- Obsession has an ugly face

- The face in the mirror/ barring teeth in your direction

- Smiles through jagged cracks/ getting the best of you

- Obsession has an ugly face/ while I don't understand

- I can plainly see that this is the disease that devours you

- The ugly face of obsession.

Story of Darkness

2008

- The sun sets violently against the tree tops
- Weighted down by the waking trees
- Colors fade into one another- art in the making
- The canvas skies lay submissive to creation
- The roads move beneath us- roads to nowhere- leading to a somewhere nothing
- Bridges crossed- skies afire
- I sink beneath thought and watch the darkness take over
- Tales of a scorched heart and bleeding emotions struggle for room in my mind
- Moments from the world being engulfed in blackness
- My soul hungrily awaits the calm- chained to fate- I wait
- A fictional character created by a sad six year old boy.

Different Sort of View

2009

- The words I bleed from the voice you see

- Blinded by the disappointments in me

- Angry at the shadows for concealing the truth

- Yet running from the sun- held back by a noose

- A fantasy straw to drain the poison from the wound

- Never over doing it- not stopping too soon

- Just rake the eyes of clarity and tell another lie

- Fixated on a reflection- tormented am I

- It's only a fragment of who I am now

- I shackled the beast- and I'll tell you how

- A moon so bright and a sun so pure

- The two factors that helped me endure

- Placed in a mold that is a perfect fit

- Thank God I didn't give up... you never let me quit
- Now I face tomorrow with a different sort of view
- I am only here because of the two of you

Taken for Granted Life

2009

- Angels and separated limbs fill the blanket skies of lavender and lies
- Believe in salvation through the broken ribs of failure
- Learn to live, love, and die with the passion your dreams are made of
- Kill off the regret that shackles down your happiness
- Throw caution to the wind and do not squander opportunities
- End your day with the thankfulness that you were able to end your day
- Someone wasn't so lucky
- Take for granted nothing that brings you the slightest smile
- It may not always be there
- Climb the crooked spine of the world and place your bets
- Life is not what you make it- but rather, how you take it

- Calm your angry eyes and unclench your fists
- Break the legs of fate to reach your goal
- As life sometimes puts things out of reach
- And lastly, peer into the mirror
- Don't let that one get you.

Mr. Mental Block

2009

- Lost in the transparent, self absorbed little steel trap I call my mind
- I struggle to find the strength to overcome this mental block
- Singled out from my former self, I stand proud and privileged- yet trying to salvage the little traits I admired
- With dull human halos and non existent wings, we gasp for clarity in our self abused minds
- Villains and misfits peer into my looking glass- my eyes- my windows to the world
- Mr. mental block himself is standing in my way
- I hold tight the strings and reserve my breaths
- For I fear the day will come when they are truly needed.

Reflection Ave.

2009

- Drive to the end of a broken hallucination
- And master escaping sorrows fascination
- Within my shadows, in a shattered reflection
- I stand clenched fists and curse my imperfections

Tyler's first poem
(As told to me by Tyler)
2009

- The moon is the mother
- The sun is the daddy
- Soon, the day will come

Perfect Strangers

2009

- Perfect strangers with a memory of the past
- A basis for comparison – hold the feeling if it lasts
- Within a mind of mass destruction, you are a peaceful thought
- In a time and place where I wasn't the same- and no battles need be fought
- A care free boy without a clue
- Overwhelmed by his feelings for you
- Wrote down on paper what he felt
- And his words made his own heart melt
- Now another time, and in another place
- I stand in the mirror- face to face
- This is the monster that waited down my path
- The sorrow and bliss- both I must have

- Remembering a decade- trials and tribulations
- Broken, lucid fascinations
- All in all, I am what I am- but never what I'll be
- And I still wonder what could have been for you and me
- But my heart beats a little faster- and a smile spreads across my face
- Our paths have taken us to a different time- a different place.

Taunting Me

2009

- Nothing can be said that hasn't been spoken
- No heart that loves hasn't been broken
- Hate with emptiness- die with passion
- Spit out broken teeth in a marketable fashion
- Sing your songs- write down your fears
- Everyone's listening with eager ears
- But you know you won't- you'll freeze and choke
- Adored only by your make believe ghost
- Fading away and being forgotten
- This is the point to which it's gotten
- And you'll be alone- if only in your head
- No one will remember you when you're dead
- As you die- broken hearted with passion
- You leave your unspoken words on paper- in your own sick fashion

Reason

2009

- Sometimes I sleep... sometimes I dream
- Sometimes I wonder what all my thoughts mean
- There's no reason to my madness... there's no logic in all the pain
- No reason to be lost in my own twisted game
- No reason to give up- no reason to try
- No reason to hold my head up high
- No reason to cry
- So I just keep going- not knowing the reason
- Enjoying ignorant bliss on the way to the reason.

Sick

2009

- Sickly sweet, translucently violent
- Tangled in my own twisted thought
- Drying and peeling from the surface of myself
- The jagged corners of my soul sticking out of my skin like broken bones
- Hand painted smiles cover my face
- The world spins- never noticing any of us
- The clock ticks swiftly as I decay with time
- Time owes me nothing...
- Gritting my teeth, fists clenched... I bare to be with myself
- Not alone in my head...
- I listen to him laugh
- Now I know it never ends
- Endure the day, endure the night
- Endure the battle, but ultimately, lose the fight

Lid Sewn Fear

2009

- Close your eyes and slip inside
- The burned edges blur your sight-close your eyes and feel alive
- Take a walk and feel the night air caress your skin with a sick kiss
- Cringe from yourself and summoning the knife
- Drag across the surface- fore play for your death
- And feel yourself come alive the closer you come to death
- Spread your lips across your face- taste your salty tears
- Close your eyes and slip inside-embraced by your darkest fears.

Road to Me

2009

- Another twisted thought/ another broken smile

- Another empty search at the end of a lonely mile

- Around sorrows grin- to the corner of shattered dreams

- One more block of salty tears- where nothing is what it seems

- Voices here comfort me/ I'm not alone inside my head

- So I wrap my thoughts in wire until the voices are dead

- Comfort is my illusion/ a dream in which I believe

- A fixation on broken thoughts/ always myself whom I deceive

- Deliver me from this evil/ my sanity wears so thin

- Reluctant to close my eyes/ darkness… the nightmare will begin

Us 1313

2009

- love is patient but life is unkind
- so many scenes I want to rewind
- play them back so I do not falter
- fast forward to when I'm at the alter
- joined hands/ it's meant to be
- my heart knowing she's the one for me
- feeling the pain of our past mistakes
- making it right no matter what it takes
- love is forgiving/ it does not judge
- I push- but the man in the mirror won't budge
- I push him away to embrace love
- His hands grasping my throat- I've had enough
- Love compromises/ real love is grand
- Holding sorrow in the palm of my hand
- Squeeze it away/ wash it in the rain
- Help me let go of the torment and pain
- Love is patient and so am I
- She has my heart till the day I die.

Spread the Fear

2009

- The clock strikes ten and I'm almost out of breath
- Using my bitter words to beat my mind to death
- A monotone glare from the grin on the other side
- Losing self control and going along for the ride
- Wicked smiles and shiny eyes tempt the fingers of fate
- Wandering minds drown in pools of thought the longer we seem to wait
- Our procrastination- our enemy- we lose before we begin
- Running circles in our minds- lost and lonely within
- Spread my panic/ spread my fear
- Spread my darkness with words to your ear
- Gift you my sorrow, sadness, and guilt

- Lies decaying the foundation you've built
- Losing your balance and falling from grace
- Look in my face to see your disgrace
- Into my eyes/ into the fear
- Stealing away the faith you hold dear
- Like numbers on your neck- your soul is imprinted
- Scattered about- tortured and demented
- Bleeding from your mouth the words you've lost
- I've spread my fear at all your costs.

Metamorphosis pt. 1
2009

- This is me, becoming alive
- Opening my eyes for the very first time
- Feeling something I've never felt before
- Bittersweet smiles as I open this door
- It's always a struggle- but I've gained new life
- And now I smile at what used to be strife
- I'm giving in to something greater
- I owe my life to God- my creator
- In my words are tangled emotions
- A beautiful symphony of twisted devotions
- My smile seems to stick- it will not fade
- As I see life as it's made
- Choices and decisions- love and regret
- It will get as good as I let it get
- God watches over us as I try to do right
- Gaining faith and not losing sight
- It feels so good- it feels so new
- I owe my changes all to you.

Metamorphosis pt. 2

2009

- In the end I'll find my way
- Based on the decisions that I make
- No matter what, you've changed who I am
- Turing my head towards the light/ opening my eyes
- Growing stronger under Gods skies
- Everything gets better, and I'm starting to heal
- Couldn't stand the way I would feel
- Now I'm looking for guidance from above
- I hope I can amount to enough
- Is it love that has a name?
- No matter what- I am about to change.

Metamorphosis pt.3
2009

- I have no idea why it took so long to see
- All the love you have for me
- So many emotions flow through my heart
- Escaping the loneliness that tore me apart
- To sacrifice your son to save my life- just to see me turn my back
- I pray for your forgiveness- I'm never going back
- You have blessed my life in so many ways
- I cannot contain my emotions these past few days
- All my tears- I shed in shame
- For taking so long to love your name
- You've always been here- by my side
- I'm sorry it took so long to open my eyes

- Now that I'm living my life for you
- Stand by me in my battles- help me stay true
- Hold me in your arms- now- and until the end
- Until my life after this one begins
- This life is a pair of shoes I walk in on my way home
- With you in my life, I will never be alone
- Thank you for my life, my strength, your love
- Until I find my place... with you up above.

Paint the Blackened Skies

2010

- Blackened skies cannot halt me on my path
- Spirit led- ignoring the lurking evil
- Attempts to lure me and seduce me away
- Righteous anger builds as my faith grows
- Dare to run; break the earthly chains
- Coming in dreams to remind me of the struggles
- Yet a losing effort is left in your hands
- Curse the blackened skies and paint them blue
- A soldier of spiritual warfare rests at his saviors feet
- Love- the unbreakable bond- does not give way to evil
- Try another day- yet know- nothing overcomes the power of his name.

I Need You
2010

- To put all I have into every breath you gave me

- All you are- I wasn't worthy- still you saved me

- To live for you- knowing that my past is behind me- more than I could ever pray for

- All the world needs you my savior

- He who knew no sin took the nails for me

- To die and rise again to set me free

- And I will sing your praises and shout your name

- Jesus- you are the one

- And everyday I need you

- And everyday I need to/ know you/ and show you/ how much I really love you.

Hope

2010

- There is a hope/ a light that shine sin the darkness
- There is a hand when you feel you can't get up
- There is guidance when you know you've lost your way
- There is your savior, Jesus, loving everyday
- There was a sacrifice that saved you from your sin
- There was a body that bleed for your mistakes
- There is a God that will forgive you
- There is your savior, Jesus, waiting for you
- Emptiness- replaced with your love
- All my regrets- replaced with your love
- And it took so long for me to see
- How much my savior did for me

- And with my back turned he continued to care
- Hard to express the love I share
- To know Jesus in all his glory
- Gods love is more than a story
- And ' Jesus saves' is the understatement of the year
- The love of Christ knows no fear
- I will continue to worship, and pray, and thank you everyday
- Giving you my life for the debt I can't repay
- Christ, my savior, hold me in your arms/ your grace sets me free

Come Alive

2010

- Engulf me in divine love
- Like only can be given from up above
- Mercy and forgiveness is bliss in my heart
- I know you've been with me from the start
- To love and obey; to fear your name
- Love and the man are one and the same
- Jesus became flesh- saved me from my sin
- Rescued me from the torment I was in
- God is love; Christ is the way
- Thank him for his sacrifice each and everyday
- Salvation at your door, won't you let him in?
- Let him save you from the sin you're living in
- Open your heart/ truth you shall receive
- Open your eyes/ you need to believe.

Masked

2010

- I never saw through your mask
- Never spoke the words you needed
- Never showed love where the lord would have had me show
- My failure will haunt me; but drive me the same
- God as my strength, I will shout his name
- You've left behind saddened hearts
- God heals all
- Father, guide us; sheep so lost in the dark
- Bring us home to your arms
- Your mask wore a smile that fooled us all
- I wish I had really known you
- I feel as though I failed you; we all failed you
- In your end, a lesson has been taught
- Tell them all- glory to God!
- Saddened hearts will heal in time
- You will be missed.

Letter from your Servant

2010

- To God on high, I stand in awe
- All knowing God, you see every flaw
- Cut open and my weakness shown
- Yet you love me with the greatest love I've ever known
- So fragile, so weak; I am so wrong
- Most powerful God, you make me feel strong
- Your mercy- a blanket that covers my heart
- Help me, oh lord, to play my part
- To reach out to those in need
- To let you use me as you please
- Christ, my savior, bring me to my knees
- And let my actions speak
- Until the whole world sees

Descended Love

2010

- Descended upward/ without notice, you were gone
- Hearts left with a void
- Grace of God be my strength
- Holding my saviors hand as he leads me through fields of pain…
- Teary eyes created by loss
- Clinging to fond memories of descended loved ones gone before me
- Watching over me with love
- Gods hand moves so swiftly
- In righteous ways he molds his world
- Even through heartache we praise his name
- Gods love heals all
- So many memories/ so much love
- Loss- a hard pill to swallow
- Visions of your smile comfort me

- Memories of your voice- like music to my heart
- Cherished memories- stored forever
- Life fades ever so quickly- like that of a fog- lifted and gone
- Descended to heaven where our lord dwells
- Finding home in the kingdom of God
- I dream of open arms awaiting me.

Journey
2010

- Another sun rises, as none are promised
- It is amazing- who you are
- An undeniable, overwhelming love pushes out fear
- I feel you in the wind…as you give me strength to stand
- Arming me appropriately for the battle at hand
- Lord, you alone are my fortress
- Rescue me from me as the trials of life crash like waves against me
- Lead me from the temptation of the enemy
- And let me find shelter under your mighty wings.

Eyes to See

2010

- Pry open blind eyes and help me see

- The plans you have in store for me

- Let me not overlook an open door

- Turn sinners hands into something more

- Almighty God- the one true power

- Save me now in this darkest hour

- For every hour without you is pitch black

- Forgive my sins and take me back

- Into your loving arms and set me free

- Help me view the world as you see

- Help me to love, and live to serve you

- And find my place in your house when this life is through

Don't Let Go

2010

- From the edge I slip, and you grab my hand
- Pull me up and together we stand
- Don't let go/ I can't walk on my own
- I cannot survive this life alone
- Daily struggles eat at me without you near
- Tortured by pain and consumed by fear
- Your light guides my way through the darkness I'm in
- Fills me with love and saves me from sin
- Don't let go; my grip is too weak
- Help me find the paths I seek
- Fill me with your love and bend me to your will
- You who won't forsake me; by my side still.

Towards Heaven

2010

- All around me shines your light
- Helping me to prepare for the fight
- I have the same tongue/ now it only speaks truth
- Not to waste it as I did in my youth
- Speak the word of God to your fellow man
- Remind them all that God has a plan
- For me and you and all the rest
- Our father in heaven only wants what's best
- Do not be embarrassed/ shed your shame
- Praise God and his holy name
- Remove your mask and be set free
- Shine your light for the world to see
- I've broken away from all my disaster
- I'm still running/ but now much faster
- Towards a destination/ God/ my rock

- Just one sheep in his very large flock
- I'm only one but he loves me so much
- My life was meaningless without his touch
- So open your eyes and come alive
- Join me now on heavens ride
- On our way to the kingdom of God
- Leading the way with his staff and his rod
- Follow the footsteps of Jesus, our king
- Join hands and together we sing
- As I have said- the path has been paved
- Only by Jesus- we all have been saved.

The Overflow
2010

- Choose your reaction to lifes situations
- Praying your way through the complications
- Your positive attitude can be contagious
- To spill that on another would be so gracious
- A hard blue surface with soft pages in the middle
- No need to decipher ; a book is my riddle
- Written words of God, put down in print
- About the perfect son that our God sent
- To save us all/ to die on the cross
- I shed a tear for the worlds greatest loss
- Your cup runs over/ filled up like the ocean

- The overflow effect is set into motion
- Starting with the person next to you, it begins to spread
- You will be judged by every word you have said
- You can change the world/ it starts in your heart
- And that's not the end of it
- It's only just the start.

Like I have previously said… most of what is in this collection is the me I would often like to forget.

But to look back and see how far God has carried me is amazing. This collection is a testimony to that. It is my transformation… from the man I was to the man I have become.

I feel like, without an example of the darkness in which I dwelled, the light wouldn't shine as bright… understand?

It is only because of Jesus Christ, my lord and savior, that I am who I am today… all the glory to God.

I know God is far from done with me… or you for that matter… he has plans specifically made for each of us! We should be flattered beyond belief. Salvation is attainable, for our lord Jesus has paid our debt… thank you lord- for all you do and for all that you are.

It is my sincerest hopes that when someone reads this poetry they will be able to say- that is ALL GOD- because I honestly can't take credit for anything good in my life… It has all been God. God bless you all… all of you who put up with and stuck by me in the tough times…and for everyone else in my life today… God bless.

- Mickey

www.ingramcontent.com/pod-product-compliance
Lightning Source LLC
Chambersburg PA
CBHW021223090426
42740CB00006B/350